GREAT TRIALS OF THE TWENTIETH CENTURY™

THE MISSISSIPPI BURNING TRIAL

JUL 0 8 2004

A Primary Source Account

Bill Scheppler

rosen central
Primary Source™

The Rosen Publishing Group, Inc., New York

Published in 2004 by The Rosen Publishing Group, Inc.
29 East 21st Street, New York, NY 10010

Unless otherwise attributed, all quotes in this book are excerpted from court transcripts.

Library of Congress Cataloging-in-Publication Data

Scheppler, Bill.
The Mississippi burning trial : a primary source account/by Bill Scheppler.—1st ed.
     v. cm.—(Great trials of the twentieth century)
Includes bibliographical references.
Contents: Understanding Mississippi in the 1960s—The victims—The defendants—
Piecing together the crime—In the courtroom—Jury deliberation and
the verdict.
ISBN 0-8239-3972-3
1. Trials (Murder)—Mississippi—Meridian. 2. Murder—Mississippi—Neshoba
County—History—20th century. 3. Civil rights workers—Crimes against—
Mississippi—Neshoba County—History—20th century. 4. Goodman, Andrew,
1943–1964. 5. Chaney, James Earl, 1943–1964. 6. Schwerner, Michael Henry,
1939-1964. [1. Trials (Murder) 2. Murder. 3. Civil rights workers. 4. Goodman,
Andrew, 1943–1964. 5. Chaney, James Earl, 1943–1964. 6. Schwerner, Michael
Henry, 1939–1964.]
I. Title. II. Series: Great trials of the 20th century.

KF224.M47S34 2004
345.73'02523'09762685—dc21

2002153811

CONTENTS

FREEDOM SUMMER MURDERS

On June 21, 1964, voting rights activists James Chaney, Andrew Goodman, and Michael Schwerner, who had come here to investigate the burning of Mt. Zion Church, were murdered. Victims of a Klan conspiracy, their deaths provoked national outrage and led to the first successful federal prosecution of a civil rights case in Mississippi.

MISSISSIPPI DEPARTMENT OF ARCHIVES AND HISTORY, 1989

Donated by the listeners of WKXI, Jackson, MS

Outside the reconstructed Mt. Zion Church in Neshoba County, Mississippi, stands this plaque. It commemorates the lives of three young men who were murdered by the Ku Klux Klan in June 1964 for their involvement in the civil rights movement. The church was being used as a freedom school for blacks that summer and was burned to the ground by the Klan. The FBI field inspector who led the investigation into the deaths of the three activists coined the term "Mississippi Burning" in reference to the burning of the church.

INTRODUCTION

In the twenty-first century, it is difficult to imagine a United States of America without equal rights for all citizens. When reciting the Pledge of Allegiance, we conclude with the words "liberty and justice for all" not "liberty and justice for all white male landowners." Yet this was exactly the case from the time of the country's founding until December 18, 1865, with the adoption of the Thirteenth Amendment to the Constitution of the United States. Proposed on January 31, 1865—two months before the end of the Civil War—the Thirteenth Amendment sought to make slavery a federal crime in the United States, punishable by force.

In order for a proposed amendment to become law, it must be ratified, or agreed to, by three-quarters of the states. The Thirteenth Amendment achieved this goal on December 6, 1865, without the support of the state of Mississippi, which rejected the amendment on December 4, 1865.

One hundred and thirty years after its proposal, the Thirteenth Amendment still had not received ratification from Mississippi. In quiet rebellion, Mississippi state leaders were making a defiant statement to the rest of the country that equal rights were not an entitlement in

Mississippi. Furthermore, Mississippi refused to be influenced by the power of the federal government.

In 1964, it would have been difficult to imagine a more dangerous place for an outsider to launch the next wave in the civil rights movement. On a late summer evening in that pivotal year, in that state full of defiance, three civil rights workers—Mickey Schwerner, Andrew Goodman, and James Chaney—were gunned down on an isolated dirt road in Neshoba County, Mississippi.

UNDERSTANDING MISSISSIPPI IN THE 1960s

The crime that spurred the "Mississippi Burning" trial took place in 1964, a year in which the social climate in the United States was ripe for a violent attack on good-intentioned individuals. In the early 1960s, much of the country was enjoying the sense of optimism instilled by President John F. Kennedy and his administration. During Kennedy's brief time in office, he founded the Peace Corps, appointed NAACP (National Association for the Advancement of Colored People) legal director Thurgood Marshall to the U.S. Court of Appeals, and drafted the Civil Rights Act, which was signed into law by his successor, President Lyndon B. Johnson. Energized by the promise of a bright future, young adults across the country, particularly college students, lined up to participate in programs they believed would contribute to America's progress.

Such progress, however, was not on the minds of all Americans. In the South, leaders in states such as Mississippi and Alabama were struggling to preserve a way of life that had not changed much in the last hundred years. Although the Emancipation Proclamation of 1863

THE CIVIL RIGHTS ACT OF 1964

The Civil Rights Act of 1964 was an attempt by President Lyndon B. Johnson (above) and the federal government to improve the quality of life for African Americans. This single legislative act addressed civil rights in five key areas:

- Outlawed unequal application requirements for voter registration

- Prohibited discrimination in public facilities, such as restaurants and hotels, that engaged in interstate commerce

- Encouraged desegregation of public schools, giving the U.S. attorney general the power to enforce this desegregation

- Authorized the withdrawal of federal funds from programs practicing discrimination

- Banned employment discrimination in businesses exceeding twenty-five workers and created an Equal Employment Opportunities Commission to review complaints

abolished the practice of slavery in the United States, racism remained and had a strong hold in the South. This state-sponsored racial inequality was a target of civil rights activists. As the movement grew stronger, the guilty parties became more desperate.

Segregationists were dealt their first major blow on May 17, 1954, when the U.S. Supreme Court, ruling in the case of *Brown v. Board of Education of Topeka, Kansas,* deemed racial segregation of public schools unconstitutional. The ruling helped trigger a revival of the Ku Klux Klan (KKK) in the region, as whites moved to retain control. But their efforts were in vain: The civil rights movement continued to gain momentum.

Tensions were high in the 1960s, as seen in this photo taken outside a Maryland restaurant on July 9, 1963. Despite the fact that this sit-in protesting segregation in public places was supposed to be peaceful, owner Robert Fehsenfeldt smashed an egg into the face of a demonstrator.

THE FREEDOM RIDES

Brown v. Board of Education reversed an 1896 Supreme Court decision in the case of *Plessy v. Ferguson*, which introduced the "separate but equal" concept. "Separate but equal" meant blacks and whites were equal in the eyes of the law, but the law would not force the two races to function together in society. It was during this time that many facilities such as drinking fountains, washrooms, and lunch counters were labeled "Whites Only" and "Colored."

The *Brown v. Board of Education* decision was welcomed by southern blacks, but segregationists unwilling to accept the Supreme Court's ruling

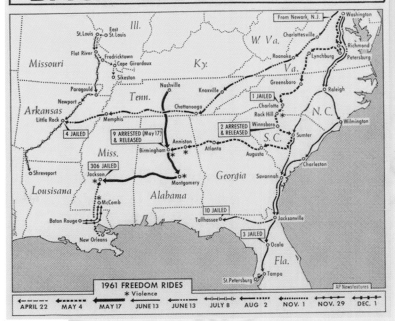

BACKGROUND MAP

1961 FREEDOM RIDES
* Violence

AP Newsfeatures

APRIL 22   MAY 4   MAY 17   JUNE 13   JUNE 13   JULY 8   AUG 2   NOV. 1   NOV. 29   DEC. 1

continued to refuse blacks access to whites-only facilities. It was as if nothing had changed.

In 1960, black college students formed the Student Nonviolent Coordinating Committee (SNCC) and began holding sit-ins at segregated lunch counters to protest the disregard for *Brown v. Board of Education*. A typical sit-in would have a small group of blacks, and sometimes white sympathizers, sit at a whites-only lunch counter and ask for service. Usually, they would not be served but were instead taunted and even beaten by angry groups of whites. Nevertheless, SNCC members refused to fight back. The idea behind the protests was to bring attention to the discrimination black people faced on a daily basis without escalating the violence.

Sit-ins evolved into "wade-ins" at segregated public beaches, "read-ins" at libraries, and eventually the freedom rides, or "sit-ins on wheels" as described by James Farmer, the national director of the Congress for Racial Equality (CORE).

The freedom rides were in direct response to a 1960 Supreme Court ruling declaring it unconstitutional to segregate interstate bus terminals. Thirteen CORE volunteers participated in the first freedom ride from Washington, D.C., to New Orleans. Their goal was to desegregate the terminals at the stops along the route simply by sitting in waiting rooms and using washroom facilities. Like the SNCC activists, they would respond to any conflict with nonviolence.

Top: Freedom riders, a group sponsored by the Congress of Racial Equality (CORE), recuperate after fleeing their burning bus on May 14, 1961, in Anniston, Alabama. The bus was the target of a white mob that stoned the vehicle, slashed its tires, and set it on fire. Freedom riders had to deal with ongoing terrorism from racist whites during their drives across the United States. *Bottom:* The 1961 Freedom Rides Background Map, which indicates areas of violence, arrests, and imprisonments.

11

The trip began peacefully enough until two freedom riders were assaulted at a terminal in Rock Hill, South Carolina. Following that incident, word of the protest spread through the South. In Georgia, a mob gathered to meet the freedom riders but missed the bus by several hours. At Anniston, the first Alabama stop, the riders were severely beaten by a waiting gang of segregationists. A few miles north of Birmingham, Alabama, freedom riders were arrested in order to avoid a repeat of Anniston. The riders insisted on continuing their trek, however, and ultimately arrived at the Birmingham station, where they were attacked by 200 to 300 people.

Attorney General Robert Kennedy advised the freedom riders not to cross the border into Mississippi because the federal government could offer no protection. Predictably, the riders refused to back down, so Kennedy appealed to Mississippi senator James Eastland to guarantee their safety. The bus rolled across the state line under armed escort of the Mississippi National Guard and was met only by reporters and police upon its arrival in Jackson. Violence was sidestepped for the time being, but the civil rights movement had officially arrived in Mississippi.

CRACKING OLE MISS

In January 1961, twenty-nine-year-old James Meredith applied for enrollment at the University of Mississippi at Oxford (nicknamed Ole Miss). However, despite *Brown v. Board of Education*, Ole Miss remained a segregated institution, and Meredith was black. By May, Meredith had been rejected by Ole Miss admissions twice. He received stock reasons for his rejections, such as missing the application deadline. Meredith believed the refusals were due to his race, so he contacted the NAACP Legal Defense and Educational Fund.

The NAACP immediately sued Mississippi's Board of Trustees of the Institutions of Higher Learning, but the state stalled the case for

Photographer Flip Schulke captured this image of Lieutenant Governor Paul Johnson Jr. *(center, wearing hat)* blocking James Meredith from walking onto the University of Mississippi campus in Oxford, Mississippi, on September 26, 1962. Meredith initiated integration at Ole Miss by becoming the first black student to be admitted to the university. In anticipation of a fight over his presence, he was accompanied by U.S. attorney John Doar *(facing out, center)* and United States marshall James McShane *(standing to right, arms crossed)*.

more than a year, doing everything it could to dismiss the case or at least delay it indefinitely. Finally, on September 10, 1962, U.S. Supreme Court justice Hugo Black handed down an order demanding that Ole Miss admit Meredith in time for the start of the fall semester. But that wasn't the end of it. Mississippi governor Ross Barnett pledged to fight the order, vowing to go to prison before submitting to the federal government.

James Meredith arrived at the Ole Miss campus on September 30 under the protection of 450 federal marshals. A riot erupted. Twenty-five thousand National Guard troops, hundreds of injuries, two deaths, and one day later, Meredith registered for class.

Meredith's victory was another blow for Mississippi segregationists. They resented the federal government for forcing the state to change its policies, and they felt abandoned by their state leaders who had vowed to stand up to outside pressure. Ordinary citizens felt the time had come to take matters into their own hands.

MOCK ELECTIONS

The integration of lunch counters, bus stations, and schools drew global attention to the problem of institutionalized racism in the southern United States, but the doors it opened for blacks in Mississippi were not yet safe enough to pass through easily. As long as state leaders accepted segregation and looked the other way when vigilante mobs used violence to deny civil rights, life would not improve for southern blacks. The answer had to be active participation in the electoral process.

In 1962, the Council of Federated Organizations (COFO) brought together SNCC, CORE, and NAACP members to launch a voter registration drive. Once blacks were made aware that voting was an option for them and learned how to prepare for a voter registration test, they could replace segregationists with political representatives who held their best interests at heart. Then they could begin to make true progress.

Unfortunately, the white Mississippians in power made it very difficult (often impossible) for blacks to pass a voter registration test. Intimidation played a role in discouraging blacks from registering and voting, resulting in an inspired but unsuccessful campaign.

Allard Lowenstein, a well-known activist, came up with an idea that could demonstrate the potential success of the program: COFO

A civil rights activist teaches elderly black voters how to fill out their voting ballots in Alabama, in this photograph taken by Flip Schulke. It was discovered that many African Americans were being disqualified from voting, simply because their ballots were filled out incorrectly. This effectively took voting power away from the black public.

would run its own candidate against hard-line segregationist Paul Johnson in the governor's election of 1963. Run exactly as a legitimate campaign, Lowenstein's plan was a mock election, which allowed black voting-age adults to mark "freedom ballots" from the safety of their own homes without registering first. By election night on November 4, 1963, more than 80,000 people voted using freedom ballots. Lowenstein had proven that, given the opportunity, blacks were ready to participate in the electoral process.

In order to staff the mock election, Lowenstein recruited sixty student volunteers. Almost immediately following the election, plans were put into place to broaden the voter registration drive in the summer of 1964. The result was the Mississippi Summer Project, a program designed to bring up to two thousand student volunteers to the Magnolia State to support widespread civil rights activity. In cities across the state, police departments prepared for the project by increasing their resources in both manpower and firepower.

THE VICTIMS

The three civil rights workers who were murdered on the evening of June 21, 1964, didn't know each other well; they had only recently met. But they shared a commitment to improving the lives of blacks throughout the South. They came from different backgrounds, and each brought his own strengths to the civil rights movement.

MICKEY SCHWERNER

Twenty-four-year-old Michael "Mickey" Schwerner and his wife of less than two years, Rita, arrived in Meridian, Mississippi, from New York City on January 24, 1964. The two were hired as CORE field staff workers to establish a community center where, among other activities, Lauderdale County residents could gather socially, take classes to develop employment skills, and prepare for voter registration. Schwerner's experience as a social worker made him ideally suited for the assignment.

But the passionate and determined Schwerner believed he could do much more to further the civil rights movement in Meridian. A man of

The FBI began distributing this photograph of Mickey Schwerner after Schwerner disappeared on June 21, 1964. Born in New York in 1939, Schwerner graduated from Cornell University in 1961 and then married Rita Levant. They joined CORE together, supporting its pacifist (antiwar) beliefs and the influences of writer Henry David Thoreau and civil rights leader Mahatma Gandhi.

action, he was convinced he could combat racism by working directly with people. In Meridian, Schwerner put this philosophy to work. Many locals warned him of the dangers of moving too quickly.

By late February, the Meridian Community Center was up and running, and Schwerner had moved on to other projects. He worked to integrate segregated churches, to remove "Whites Only" and "Colored" signs from public facilities, and to encourage blacks to vote. But his most visible project was the organization of a boycott of three five-and-ten stores that did business in black communities while refusing to hire black employees. The boycott began in April, and by the first week of June, one of the stores hired a black woman who was trained as a sales clerk at the community center. Schwerner was proud of his achievement, but the locals' warnings were accurate.

To Lauderdale County segregationists, especially members of the KKK and law enforcement officers, Mickey Schwerner was the most hated man in Mississippi, black or white. He was an outsider, and his actions to improve civil rights were a threat to their way of life. Sam Bowers was the imperial wizard of the Mississippi Knights of the Ku Klux Klan in 1964, and in the second week of May, he gave the order for Schwerner's murder.

JAMES CHANEY

A Meridian native, James Chaney was more than aware of the roles of blacks and whites in southern society. Like most black families in Mississippi, the Chaneys had firsthand knowledge of the severity of punishment when a black person challenged those roles. At least two members of Chaney's extended family had "come up missing" following run-ins with white men. James Chaney understood exactly how to behave in order to survive in a segregated society, but he also had the courage to work for a better world.

Chaney was introduced to the civil rights movement as a high school student. He and his friends attended NAACP meetings and wore paper NAACP badges to school to flaunt their support. The school principal perceived their actions as controversial and suspended the boys for a week when they refused orders to remove the badges.

In 1963, twenty-year-old Chaney didn't have much going on in his life. He had been expelled from high school, was rejected by the U.S. Army, and was living at home with his mother and four siblings. A

Slain civil rights worker James Chaney is shown in this photograph, taken in Meridian, Mississippi. Twenty-one-year-old Chaney proved to be an indispensable member of CORE. The Schwerners' letter to CORE headquarters asking that Chaney become a paid staff member stated, "We consider him to be part of the Meridian staff . . . James has never asked us to buy him a cup of coffee, though he has no means."

friend introduced him to Matt Suarez, the CORE staff member assigned to start up a local movement. Suarez was a twenty-five-year-old U.S. Navy veteran from New Orleans. Chaney was immediately drawn to him and became an enthusiastic volunteer.

Suarez brought the Schwerners to Meridian to build the community center, and Chaney was there from day one. Chaney was invaluable to

Schwerner's plans for Mississippi. As a black man, he could more easily gain the trust of other black citizens whom Schwerner wanted to reach. He was also a skilled driver and was familiar with eastern Mississippi's back roads, which meant he could escape dangerous situations—fast. And he was an expert adviser on local residents and their customs. The Schwerners so respected Chaney's contributions to their work that they wrote to the CORE national office in April, recommending him for a full-time position.

ANDREW GOODMAN

Andrew Goodman met Mickey Schwerner and James Chaney during the first phase of the Mississippi Summer Project, a weeklong training program held in Ohio. Schwerner was immediately impressed with Goodman's intelligence and composure, and he attempted to recruit the twenty-year-old student to spend the summer working with Chaney to establish a freedom school at the Mount Zion Church in Longdale, Mississippi, where blacks of all ages could learn traditional subject matter as well as black history. However, Goodman had already decided on a different assignment. He was looking forward to helping civil rights veteran Eric Weinberger set up a leatherworking cooperative in Canton, Ohio.

Goodman viewed the Mississippi Summer Project as a learning experience. Although he was a student of the civil rights movement and agreed with its principles, he was not committed to it as his life's work. Goodman, who enjoyed a privileged upbringing, simply wanted to spend the summer doing something significant and give back to people less fortunate than himself. Before signing up for the project, he had considered joining the "Mexican Volunteers" program to spend the summer building a school in an impoverished barrio outside of Mexico City.

This photo, taken June 15, 1964, in Oxford, Ohio, shows Andrew Goodman attending a meeting as part of a three-day training session for the Mississippi Summer Project. Goodman, who died at the age of twenty, grew up in a liberal household on the Upper West Side of New York City. Visitors to his parents' home included convicted communist spy Alger Hiss and blacklisted actor Zero Mostel.

Later in the week of the summer project, word of beatings and arson at Mount Zion Church reached Schwerner in Ohio. Schwerner was more determined than ever to establish the freedom school in order to prove the Ku Klux Klan could not scare him off, but he also realized he needed the aid of a superior volunteer. He approached Goodman one final time about taking the position, and this time the young man accepted. Early the next morning, Mickey Schwerner, James Chaney, and Andrew Goodman piled into the blue CORE station wagon and headed south for Mississippi.

THE DEFENDANTS

No one has ever been charged for the murders of Mickey Schwerner, James Chaney, and Andrew Goodman. But on December 4, 1964, after more than five months of intensive investigation by the Federal Bureau of Investigation (FBI), the U.S. Justice Department arrested nineteen men from Lauderdale and Neshoba Counties for depriving the three victims of their civil rights.

The defendants were not charged with murder because a murder trial must be prosecuted by the state in which the crime was committed, with a state circuit judge residing over the hearing. Due to the widespread racism in Mississippi at the time, the Justice Department did not believe a murder conviction was possible. In addition, the civil rights violations with which the defendants were charged are federal crimes. Mississippi officials would have less control over the proceedings, and the prosecution would have a better chance of winning.

On December 10, Esther Carter, U.S. commissioner for the Southern District of Mississippi, dismissed the charges against all the defendants after ruling the testimony of a key prosecution witness hearsay evidence

THE CHARGES

itle 18, Section 241—Conspiracy Against Rights. "If two or more persons conspire to injure, oppress, threaten, or intimidate any person . . . in the free exercise or enjoyment of any right or privilege secured to him by the Constitution . . . or if two or more persons go in disguise on the highway, or on the premises of another, with intent to prevent . . . free exercise or enjoyment of any right or privilege," they are in violation of this law.

Title 18, Section 242—Deprivation of Rights Under Color of Law. "Whoever, under color of any law, statute, ordinance, regulation, or custom, willfully subjects any person . . . to the deprivation of any rights [or] privileges . . . secured . . . by the Constitution . . . or to different punishments, pains, or penalties, on account of such person being an alien, or by reason of his color, or race," is in violation of Title 18, Section 242.

because it was disclosed to a single FBI agent. Clearly an attempt to sabotage the trial, Carter's action was a typical example of Mississippi's severe contempt for the federal government.

Following two lengthy defense-initiated delays, one of which was appealed all the way to the U.S. Supreme Court, the trial finally began on October 9, 1967. Between December 1964 and the start of the trial, the prosecution dropped five defendants from the original case and added four new names. Ultimately, the following eighteen men stood trial for violating Title 18, Sections 241 and 242 of the U.S. Criminal Code.

BERNARD AKIN

Longtime Klansman Bernard Akin owned Akin's Mobile Homes in Meridian, a frequent Klan meeting spot. The outspoken fifty-eight-year-old was too visible in Lauderdale County to take part in the lynching, but that didn't stop the perpetrators from gathering at his place on the afternoon of June 21 to hatch their final plan.

JIMMY ARLEDGE

A twenty-seven-year-old Meridian truck driver, Jimmy Arledge was exactly the type of person the Klan depended on to execute its violent actions. Arledge was full of anger and youthful energy, and he was hungry for the respect of the older Klansmen. He welcomed the opportunity to take part in the June 21 murders.

ETHEL "HOP" BARNETT

Hop Barnett preceded Lawrence Rainey as Neshoba County sheriff and was every bit as ruthless as his successor. It was Hop who noticed the lively gathering at Mount Zion Church on June 16 and encouraged the Klan to investigate, resulting in the beatings of several congregants and the burning of the church.

HORACE DOYLE BARNETTE

At the time of the murders, Doyle Barnette was a twenty-six-year-old auto parts salesman. Although he claims not to have known of the

Here are photographs of eight of the Ku Klux Klan members (one a Klan affiliate) arrested by the FBI in Mississippi on December 4, 1964. These men were arrested in connection with the murder of the three young civil rights workers. *Top, left to right:* Herman Tucker, Jimmie Snowden, Deputy Sheriff Cecil Price, Sheriff Lawrence Rainey. *Bottom, left to right:* Olen Burrage, Bernard Akin, Jimmy Lee Townsend, and Billy Wayne Posey.

Klan's plan to kill Schwerner and his companions until the last minute, Barnette played a key role in the plan's success by driving six Klansmen to Rock Cut Road.

TRAVIS BARNETTE

Travis Barnette was Doyle Barnette's half brother. At age thirty-six, he was part-owner of a Meridian garage and lived with his wife and

daughter. To a man like Travis Barnette, Klan membership provided a sense of pride. He would never amount to much, but he could always feel superior to a black man.

SAM BOWERS

Thirty-nine-year-old World War II veteran Sam Bowers established the White Knights of Mississippi branch of the Ku Klux Klan in 1963. As imperial wizard, Bowers was the leader of the Klan throughout the state, and his calling for Mickey Schwerner's elimination sealed the fate of the young civil rights worker.

OLEN BURRAGE

Olen Burrage, a respected local businessman and Klan member, owned Old Jolly Farm. He offered the farm as a burial spot for the civil rights workers just before backing out of a U.S. Department of Agriculture project that would have required periodic inspections of a cattle dam under construction on his property.

JAMES "PETE" HARRIS

As an officer in the White Knights of the KKK, Pete Harris was ineligible to directly participate in any illegal Klan activity, but he still managed to contribute. Arming himself with a telephone, Harris spent the afternoon of June 21 calling brother Klansmen and assembling a sizable lynching party.

FRANK HERNDON

Forty-six-year-old Herndon served as "cyclops," or president, of the Lauderdale klavern (local unit) and hosted Klan meetings at the Longhorn Drive-In, which he managed. Although he helped devise the plan to kill Schwerner and his companions, Herndon did not participate in the action because Klan leaders could not afford to "get their hands dirty."

Edgar Ray Killen led seventy armed men to the Mt. Zion Methodist Church in search of Mickey Schwerner. When Schwerner wasn't there, Killen and his men took out their aggressions on some black parishioners and set fire to the church to lure Schwerner back to town. This photograph was taken on December 4, 1964, the day Killen was arrested.

"PREACHER" EDGAR RAY KILLEN

Killen served as "kleagle," or organizer, for the White Knights of Mississippi, working in Lauderdale and Neshoba Counties. The local ranks of the Klan swelled in response to the arrival of Mickey and Rita Schwerner, forcing the thirty-eight-year-old ordained Baptist minister and former sheriff candidate to hold twice-weekly recruitment meetings.

BILLY WAYNE POSEY

Standing six feet three inches tall, cross-eyed with glasses, twenty-eight-year-old Billy Wayne Posey presented an unsightly yet imposing figure. Posey was an auto mechanic and a loyal member of the Neshoba klavern. Married with four children, he had the responsibility of arranging the disposal of the victims' bodies following the June 21 murders.

DEPUTY SHERIFF CECIL PRICE

Cecil Price walked in Sheriff Lawrence Rainey's shadow. Both were Klansmen, both wore cowboy apparel, and both abused their power to intimidate blacks. But on June 21, Deputy Price stepped out of the shadow. By apprehending Schwerner outside Lauderdale County, Price ignited the conspiracy that led to the Mississippi Burning trial.

SHERIFF LAWRENCE RAINEY

Lawrence Rainey, an active member of the Klan, was elected Neshoba County sheriff in 1963 amid rising tensions between residents and civil rights workers. The forty-one-year-old, eighth-grade-educated peace officer had a reputation for being tough on blacks and boasted of killing two black men in the line of duty.

WAYNE ALTON ROBERTS

A violent man even by Klan standards, twenty-six-year-old Wayne Roberts was big and mean with a short fuse. Dishonorably discharged from the U.S. Marines, Roberts eagerly joined the Klan in May 1964 and immediately began calling for Mickey Schwerner's execution. Roberts's brother, Lee, was an equally vicious Meridian police officer.

JERRY MCGREW SHARPE

Philadelphia, Mississippi, resident Jerry Sharpe was a loyal lieutenant to Ray Killen, making him one busy man. The zealous twenty-one-year-old Klansman carried out countless acts of bravado intended to both intimidate civil rights workers and attract Klan recruits. On June 21, Sharpe was perhaps the first to receive a call from Killen.

JIMMIE SNOWDEN

The evening of June 21 presented the type of opportunity for which Jimmie Snowden had been waiting. After all, the thirty-one-year-old Meridian truck driver did not join the Klan to attend meetings and burn crosses; he wanted to incite a war against integration, the civil rights movement, and Mickey Schwerner.

HERMAN TUCKER

Though not a Klansman, Herman Tucker was essential to the lynching plan. Tucker was an independent contractor who was building the cattle pond and dam on Old Jolly Farm. So when the Klan decided to bury the bodies in the dam, they called upon Tucker and his expert bulldozing skills.

RICHARD WILLIS

Richard Willis was a Klan-sympathizing Philadelphia, Mississippi, police officer who allegedly used his authority to detain and beat innocent black men on multiple occasions. Willis rode along in Deputy Cecil Price's patrol car as he escorted the three civil rights workers from the Neshoba County Jail to the city limits.

These men would stand trial in a Mississippi courtroom for a lesser crime than was actually committed. A team of twelve attorneys, divided by county into subteams, represented the defendants. In an unmistakable show of support for the Klan in Neshoba County, the entire Neshoba bar joined the defense team, including the mayor of Philadelphia, Mississippi, himself. On their home turf, with powerful town leaders defending them, the eighteen defendants thought they couldn't lose.

PIECING TOGETHER THE CRIME

After extensive investigation, lengthy witness testimony, and some connecting of dots, prosecutors painted a fairly clear picture of the events of June 21, 1964. They slowly revealed the story to jurors over the course of the trial and left the jury to decide the guilt or innocence of the defendants. To the best of our knowledge, this is what happened.

PLAN FOUR

The Master Plan for Protection of the White Knights of the KKK outlines the group's methods for dealing with people who threaten its ideals. Plan One calls for distributing leaflets and burning crosses. Plan Two includes burnings and dynamiting. Plan Three escalates to beatings and whippings. Plan Four is simple: elimination. In May 1964, during the CORE-organized boycott of white-owned Meridian businesses, Imperial Wizard Sam Bowers instructed Klansmen in Neshoba and Lauderdale Counties to activate Plan Four against Mickey Schwerner.

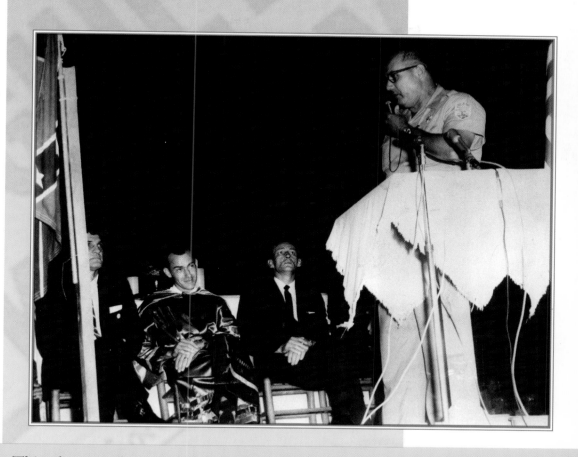

This photograph was taken on July 10, 1965 (a year after the Mississippi Burning murders) at a Ku Klux Klan rally and cross burning in Meridian, Mississippi. To the right, Neshoba County sheriff Lawrence Rainey speaks into a microphone to a crowd of about 1,500. Seated behind Rainey are *(from left)* the bodyguard of the Klan's imperial wizard; E. L. McDaniel, the grand dragon of Mississippi; and Imperial Wizard Robert Shelton.

The Klan knew Schwerner was planning to use Mount Zion Church for his next freedom school, so on the evening of June 16 when Hop Barnett reported to a Klan gathering that a meeting was in progress at the church, Klansmen armed themselves, piled into two cars, and drove to the church in search of Schwerner. Schwerner was not at the church, but the Klan decided to set a trap for him. They would burn down Mount Zion Church in an effort to lure Schwerner back to Neshoba County.

The trap worked. The morning after word of the burning reached Schwerner, he got in the blue CORE station wagon with Chaney and Goodman and drove back to Mississippi.

POLICE CUSTODY

The station wagon arrived in Meridian late on the evening of June 20. The next morning, the three civil rights workers had breakfast and prepared for the hour-long drive to Longdale, where they would investigate the remains of Mount Zion Church. They planned to arrive in Longdale at noon, spend a few hours visiting parishioners who were beaten on the night of the fire, and return to Meridian by 4:00 PM. Schwerner asked a CORE worker to call for help if they weren't back by 4:30 PM.

The afternoon went exactly as planned. The civil rights workers met a parishioner named Ernest Kirkland and got to the church by 1 PM. After assessing the damage, they visited several friends and talked about the burning and beatings. During these visits, Schwerner learned that the mob had been at the church on June 16 and was looking for him.

It is likely Schwerner took the warning seriously because the civil rights workers decided to take a longer but safer route back to Meridian. Ironically, it was on this route, traveling west on Highway 16 toward Philadelphia, Mississippi, that the station wagon passed Deputy Price heading east in his patrol car.

Price recognized the blue station wagon right away and radioed, "I've got a good one! George Raymond!" George Raymond was a black CORE worker who was despised by the Klan. Excited about the opportunity to apprehend Raymond, Price made a U-turn and gave chase. Schwerner and Goodman must have seen Price's patrol car and ducked down, and Price, detecting only a single black man driving the car, mistook Chaney for Raymond. When Chaney pulled over and Price approached the vehicle, Price was genuinely shocked to find Mickey Schwerner.

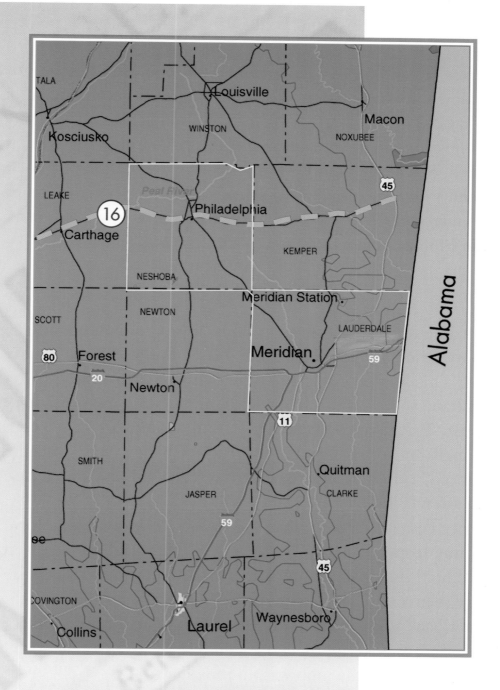

The above map shows the area of Mississippi where the events of the Mississippi Burning case took place. The town of Meridian, in Lauderdale County, was where Mickey Schwerner and his wife were dispatched to establish a community center. It was also the home of James Chaney. After visiting the Mount Zion Church, located in Neshoba County, Schwerner, Chaney, and Goodman decided to take Route 16 toward Philadelphia to Meridian, hoping to avoid the Klansmen who were reportedly after them.

Price radioed for assistance at 3:30 PM, and Mississippi State Safety Patrolmen E. R. Poe and Harry J. Wiggs answered the call. Price placed Chaney under arrest for speeding and Schwerner and Goodman for "investigation," presumably for the burning of Mount Zion Church. Schwerner and Goodman got in the backseat of Poe's patrol car, and Wiggs took the wheel of the station wagon with Chaney in the passenger seat. The two cars followed Price to the Neshoba County Jail in Philadelphia.

ASSEMBLING THE MOB

According to later testimony from jail operator Minnie Lee Herring, Deputy Price booked the civil rights workers into the county jail at 4 PM. This was precisely the time Schwerner promised to return to Meridian, so he asked to make a phone call but was denied this request. Price locked Schwerner and Goodman in a cell already occupied by Billy Charles McKay. Chaney was placed in the "Colored" cell. The deputy sheriff left the jail and would not return until after 10 PM.

Price contacted Ray Killen, the local Klan kleagle, to inform him it was time to put Plan Four into action. They laid out the plan. Price would hold the prisoners until after dark. After their release, he would follow them out of town to verify their travel route and relay the information back to the Klan. Patrolmen Wiggs and Poe would watch for the station wagon, apprehend it, and release the victims to the lynch mob. Assembling the mob was up to Killen.

Killen picked up fellow Klansmen Jerry Sharpe and Jimmy Lee Townsend (a teenager and member of the original nineteen defendants) and drove to the Longhorn Drive-In in Meridian to gather some men for the job. Frank Herndon, president of the Klan, and Pete Harris joined the group at the Longhorn and began telephoning others. After James Jordan arrived, the growing unit moved to the mobile home lot run by Bernard Akin. At this time Wayne Roberts, Jimmie Snowden, Jimmy Arledge, and the Barnette brothers, Travis and Doyle, joined the assembly.

After purchasing rubber gloves and fueling up the cars, the mob drove to Philadelphia. Klan law does not allow officers to take part in Klan action due to their visibility in the community and importance to the klavern. Therefore, Herndon, Harris, and Akin stayed in Meridian, while at 8 PM the younger members headed north on Highway 19.

ROCK CUT ROAD

Back in Philadelphia, Killen held another planning meeting with Deputy Price, Billy Wayne Posey, and Olen Burrage. They agreed on final arrangements, from the spot where the victims would be buried to the person who would operate the

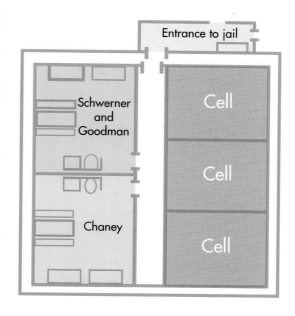

This diagram illustrates the interior of the Neshoba County Jail, where Goodman, Chaney, and Schwerner were held the evening of their murders. The three men were brought into the jail (tinted yellow), booked, and locked in two cells. Schwerner and Goodman were held in the cell tinted red, while Chaney was kept in the blue cell. The jail's telephone, which the young men were not allowed to use, sat near the entrance.

bulldozer. At 9:30 PM, Killen communicated to the lynch mob the remainder of the conspiracy. The only thing left to do was wait for the prisoners' release.

Just after 10 PM, Deputy Price entered the jail and spoke briefly with the prisoners. He then approached Minnie Lee Herring and informed her that Chaney had agreed to pay his $20 speeding fine and all three were free to go. Price released Schwerner, Chaney, and Goodman from

Taken on June 24, 1964, the above photo shows the burned CORE Ford station wagon belonging to missing activists Andrew Goodman, James Chaney, and Mickey Schwerner. The tires, windows, and interior of the car were completely ruined. Found in a swampy area, the station wagon was moved to a garage near Philadelphia, Mississippi, where FBI agents then combed the car for clues.

their jail cells, returned their belongings, and escorted them from the building. The civil rights workers did not request to use the phone upon their release.

Price and Officer Richard Willis directed the civil rights workers to their car and then climbed in Price's car and followed the station wagon to the town limits. After watching the car disappear in the distance, Price turned around and drove back to the courthouse square. Seventy-one-year-old Officer Otha Burkes relayed the station wagon's path to the members of the mob, who immediately raced south on Highway 19.

The two cars carrying the mob stopped at Pilgrim's Store, where they saw Officers Poe and Wiggs—parked! To Posey's surprise, Poe explained he had no intention of stopping the station wagon. Deputy Price joined the scene after dropping off Officer Willis. When he learned that this key element of the plan had broken down, he took matters into his own hands and at 10:25 PM sped after the station wagon.

Reaching speeds above 100 mph, the three cars gained ground on the station wagon, and with about ten miles to go to cross the Neshoba County line, Chaney noticed the patrol car and instinctively floored it. Meanwhile, Posey's 1958 Chevrolet broke down. Posey and Roberts jumped into the second car, driven by Doyle Barnette, while Sharpe and Townsend were left behind to tend to the Chevy.

Eventually, Price caught up to the station wagon and turned on his patrol car's flashing red lights. Chaney gave up the chase and pulled over. As the mob looked on, Price ordered the three out of the station wagon and into the backseat of his patrol car. When Chaney hesitated, the deputy hit him so hard on the back of his head that Jordan heard the blow from twenty yards away.

Arledge took the wheel of the station wagon, Jordan climbed into the patrol car to guard the prisoners, and Deputy Price led the caravan

This FBI missing persons poster was created on June 29, 1964. Andrew Goodman, James Chaney, and Michael Schwerner (left to right) stare out from the page. The bottoms reads: "Should you have or in the future receive any information concerning the whereabouts of these individuals, you are requested to notify me or the nearest office of the FBI. Telephone number is listed below." Signed by the director of the FBI, J. Edgar Hoover.

to a secluded dirt turnoff called Rock Cut Road. Along the way, they passed Posey's car, and Doyle Barnette picked up Sharpe.

Once the three cars parked on Rock Ridge Road, things happened pretty quickly. Roberts opened the left rear door of the patrol car, pulled Schwerner out, and asked, according to Doyle Barnette's signed statement to the FBI, "Are you that nigger-lover?" Vainly searching for a grain of decency in his accuser,

Schwerner replied, "Sir, I know just how you feel." Roberts responded by raising the gun in his right hand and firing point-blank into Schwerner's heart. Roberts returned to the car, pulled Goodman to his feet, and immediately fired a shot into his chest. When it was his turn, Chaney recognized a Meridian resident and pleaded for his life. This time, according to Barnette's confession, it was Jordan who fired, hitting Chaney in the stomach. Roberts

This photo, taken on August 5, 1964, near Philadelphia, Mississippi, shows power shovels excavating Old Jolly Farm. The FBI's major case inspector, Joseph Sullivan, received word from an anonymous source that he should investigate the site. Almost immediately, the bodies of the missing civil rights workers were unearthed. The three young men had been missing for forty-four days.

fired a second shot, which pierced Chaney's lower back, and followed it up with a bullet to the head.

The gunmen picked up their bullet casings, while the others loaded the bodies into the station wagon. It was almost 11 PM when Posey got behind the wheel of the station wagon and led the caravan to Old Jolly Farm, a 253-acre piece of land owned by Olen Burrage. There, the Klansmen took the bodies from the car, placed them near an

Four famous faces of the civil rights movement join together in a protest outside Convention Hall in Atlantic City, New Jersey, on August 24, 1964. They are (from left to right) Dr. Aaron Henry, the head of the Mississippi Freedom Democratic Party; civil rights activist Mrs. Fanny Lou Hamer; and the parents of murdered civil rights worker Mickey Schwerner.

earthen dam still under construction, and awaited bulldozer operator Herman Tucker.

When Tucker arrived, he mounted a bulldozer and scooped dirt out of the dam to create a hole large enough for the three bodies. Arledge and Posey placed the bodies in the cavity, and fifteen minutes later, Tucker expertly repaired the dam, concealing all signs of tampering.

The final step was the disposal of the station wagon. Instead of burying it with the bodies, the plan called for abandoning the car in Birmingham and torching it in the hopes of drawing the search away from the burial site. Tasked with destroying the car, Tucker only got as far as northeast Neshoba County before igniting the fire at 12:45 AM—the time the dashboard clock stopped.

WHAT ARE YOU LOOKING FOR?

Federal and state investigators probe the swampy area near Philadelphia, Mississippi, in this photograph taken by the Associated Press on June 24, 1964. The burned CORE station wagon was found at the site days after the disappearance of Schwerner, Chaney, and Goodman.

IN THE COURTROOM

C ourtroom proceedings for
the Mississippi Burning trial, or
United States v. Price et al., began on
Monday October 9, 1967, with jury selection.
At 9 AM, the white stone federal building in
Meridian buzzed with the anticipation of
reporters, witnesses, potential jurors, and specta-
tors. Judge William H. Cox immediately set strict
courtroom rules in an effort to maintain control over
the hearing.

Jury selection was relatively quick. By the end of the day,
the prosecution and defense had agreed on an all-white jury of
seven women and five men who would decide the fate of the
eighteen defendants. Opening statements were scheduled to begin
the second day's proceedings.

OPENING STATEMENTS

Prosecutor John Doar was first to address the jury. It was his job to prove
the eighteen defendants were guilty of denying the three civil rights

workers their rights. Understanding that many Mississippians resented the U.S. government for imposing its laws on their state, he took the opportunity to explain why the government had worked so hard to solve the crime. "I am here because your national government is concerned about your local law enforcement and in a civilization local law must work if we deserve our liberty and freedom," he said.

"When local law enforcement officials become involved as participants in violent crime and use their position, power, and authority to accomplish this," he continued, "there is very little to be hoped for, except with assistance from the federal government." Doar tried to convince the jury that even though the federal government was involved, the outcome was in the hands of twelve citizens from the state of Mississippi.

Assistant attorney general for civil rights John Doar was practicing law in Wisconsin when he was asked to take a job that he said "no one else wanted" in the Justice Department. A firm believer in what was right, Doar watched President Johnson sign the Voting Rights Act into law in August 1965.

In contrast to Doar's characteristically well-prepared and rational statement, the defense opened the trial with an effort to create hostility between the jury and Doar. In its opening statement, the defense attempted to portray Doar as an outsider trying to force his values on the people of Mississippi. The defense made a point of informing the jury that Doar was the spokesman for the Justice Department who had "forced the Negro James Meredith into the University of Mississippi."

WITNESS TESTIMONY

Doar and his team began presenting their case immediately following opening statements. Prosecutors called seven key witnesses whose testimony pieced together the events of June 21, 1964, leading up to the deaths of Schwerner, Chaney, and Goodman.

REVEREND CHARLES JOHNSON

The pastor of the Church of the Nazarene in Meridian and a member of the NAACP, Johnson had worked with the Schwerners in the spring of 1964. On the witness stand, he testified to the nature of the work Schwerner was assigned to do in Mississippi. Upon cross-examination, Laurel Weir of the defense team asked odd questions about Schwerner's living arrangement, religious beliefs, and views on the war in Vietnam. Although these questions seemed to have nothing to do with the case, they were part of a strategy to get the jury to recognize the civil rights workers as dangerous outsiders. Weir ignited an uproar when he asked if Johnson and Schwerner had attempted to "get young male Negroes to sign statements agreeing to rape a white woman once a week during the hot summer of 1964." Judge Cox immediately reprimanded the defense for attempting to make a farce of the trial, and the Mississippi defense team suddenly appeared vulnerable.

ERNEST KIRKLAND

A Longdale resident, member of Mount Zion Church, and Schwerner's main Neshoba County contact, Kirkland testified that he had accompanied the three civil rights workers as they investigated the charred remains of Mount Zion Church in the early afternoon of June 21.

JUDGE WILLIAM H. COX

FREEDOM SUMMER MURDERS
On June 21, 1964, voting rights activists James Chaney, Andrew Goodman, and Michael Schwerner, who had come here to investigate the burning of Mt. Zion Church, were murdered. Victims of a Klan conspiracy, their deaths provoked national outrage and led to the first successful federal prosecution of a civil rights case in Mississippi.

William Cox, Southern Mississippi District federal judge, presided over *United States v. Price et al.* President Kennedy appointed Cox, a well-known segregationist, to the bench as a favor to Mississippi senator James Eastland, who roomed with Cox during law school and now served as chairman of the Judicial Committee. In exchange, Eastland approved Kennedy's appointment of Thurgood Marshall to the U.S. Court of Appeals. The defendants believed Judge Cox would set them free, if he actually allowed the trial to take place at all.

E. R. POE

Mississippi Highway Safety Patrolman E. R. Poe testified that Deputy Sheriff Cecil Price had pulled over the blue station wagon carrying the three civil rights workers for speeding as it headed toward Lauderdale County in the afternoon of June 21. Poe stated that Deputy Price arrested all three (Chaney for speeding; Schwerner and Goodman for investigation) and requested assistance in transporting them to jail, to which Poe obliged.

47

MINNIE LEE HERRING

Minnie Lee Herring operated the Neshoba County Jail along with her husband, Virgil. On the witness stand, Minnie Lee testified that Deputy Price had booked the civil rights workers into jail at 4 PM on June 21, although he did not file tickets or conduct interviews. Deputy

In this photo taken on December 5, 1964, at their own arraignment in Meridian, Mississippi, deputy Cecil Price *(left)* and Neshoba County sheriff Lawrence Rainey *(right)* do not look at all fazed. They were arrested for the murder of the three young civil rights workers. Rainey holds a large bag of Red Man chewing tobacco and sits as though he's enjoying a movie.

Price locked up the prisoners, left the jail, and returned later that evening to permit Chaney to pay a $20 fine and thus release all three civil rights workers.

WALLACE MILLER

Sergeant Wallace Miller of the Meridian Police Department admitted his membership in the White Knights of the KKK until his banishment in December 1964. Under oath, Miller identified Wayne Roberts, Travis Barnette, Doyle Barnette, Jimmy Arledge, Pete Harris, Jimmie Snowden, Frank Herndon, Sam Bowers, Bernard Akin, and Ray Killen as members of the Klan on June 21.

Miller testified about the Klan organization as it relates to intimidation and violence, and he described the Klan's plans for Schwerner in the summer of 1964. He cited conversations after June 21 during which Herndon and Killen revealed details about the murders. Upon cross-examination, Miller declared that he never saw any of the defendants intimidate or harm the victims in any way, and he testified that when he joined the Klan, he understood it to be a patriotic and political organization made up of the county's more prominent citizens.

DELMAR DENNIS

Another Klansman, Delmar Dennis, revealed more inside information. Dennis was the first witness to identify Sheriff Rainey and Deputy Price as Klansmen. He testified that on the night of June 16, Klan members went to Mount Zion Church seeking Schwerner. Disappointed he was not present, some of the Klansmen beat the parishioners and then torched the church in hopes of luring Schwerner back to Longdale.

Dennis also testified that Price assumed James Jordan was an informant for the FBI because he was the only one who was in position to see Price hit Chaney in the back of the head on the night of June 21. He also testified to a conversation with Sam Bowers during which the imperial wizard claimed to be pleased with the job.

JAMES JORDAN

James Jordan was a Meridian Klansman who could not keep a secret. When FBI agents learned Jordan had leaked his role in the murders, they called him in for interrogation. Because Jordan was convinced the FBI had a strong case against him and he was desperate for the $3,500 paid to informants, over the course of five lengthy interviews, he told them everything he knew and became the prosecution's most valuable witness.

Though he claimed not to be an eyewitness to the shootings, Jordan played a part in the events of June 21. He gave a full account of everything he saw and heard from 6 PM to 1 AM, from gathering the lynch mob to replacing license plates on cars and disposing of rubber gloves.

HORACE DOYLE BARNETTE

Doyle Barnette's written confession was the final piece of key evidence presented by the prosecution. Barnette backed out as a witness for the prosecution, but Judge Cox allowed his confession to stand as evidence against him. Barnette was an eyewitness to the murders, so his written statement when read aloud in court completed the picture of the events of June 21.

The defense team never imagined a Mississippi jury would convict a group of white Mississippi natives, including local community leaders, in the deaths of two outsiders and a black man, so they did not take the time to prepare a strong, comprehensive case. As a result, the trial was heavily weighted in favor of the prosecution.

Klan organizer Edgar Ray Killen is shown here entering court on October 12, 1967, in Meridian, Mississippi. Delmar Dennis told the FBI that Killen said Mickey Schwerner's elimination had been approved at the Klan state level. Dennis was a personal recruit of Killen's and received $5,000 annually from the FBI to report on the activities of the Klan.

The defense's case relied upon minimal cross-examination of prosecution witnesses and character witnesses for the defendants taking the stand to confirm alibis or to uphold their reputations for honesty. These witnesses were mainly family and friends of the defendants. Over the course of the trial, jurors heard testimony from 160 witnesses. On one particularly active day, the defense called an average of one witness every seven minutes.

CLOSING ARGUMENTS

John Doar stood in front of the jury on the morning of October 18 to summarize his case against the defendants. As he did in his opening statement, Doar stressed the importance of the jury, reminding them the fate of the defendants was in the hands of Mississippians and not the federal government. "What I say, what the other lawyers say here today, what the court says about the law will soon be forgotten, but what you twelve people do here today will long be remembered," he assured the jurors.

Again Doar's presentation was delivered in a clear and controlled manner, although he did awaken some passion when speaking about the role of law enforcement in the murder plot. Pointing a finger at Price, Doar accused the deputy of employing "the machinery of his office, the badge, the car, the jail, the gun" to single-handedly ignite this powder keg of conspiracy.

The defense also closed its case in much the same way it began—with name-calling and mudslinging. Mike Watkins labeled prosecution witnesses untrustworthy paid informants. W. D. Moore accused President Johnson and his administration of instigating the investigation and claiming the federal government "opened up the coffers of the United States for money" to fund the prosecution. Herman Alford basically snubbed the entire trial proceeding, claiming the defendants were "as innocent and pure as the driven snow."

The prosecution and defense rested their cases, and at 4:24 PM on October 18, *United States v. Price et al.* was placed in the hands of the jury.

JURY DELIBERATION AND THE VERDICT

Jury deliberation in *United States v. Price et al.* was incredibly complex for many reasons. The large number of defendants made it difficult to understand each person's role in the crime and to determine the severity of one person's role in relation to another's. Because it was a conspiracy case and not a murder case, it was tricky to establish guilt. Simply knowing about the crime could constitute guilt. And it must have been terrifying to even consider convicting a member of the Klan, given their record of violence in Mississippi.

After one day of deliberation, the jury approached Judge Cox on the afternoon of October 19, claiming they could not come to a conclusion. Judge Cox told the jury a mistrial was out of the question, and he read a set of juror directions in order to encourage them to reach a verdict. Judge Cox reminded the jury how costly a trial is to the community and that a second trial would be just as costly and just as difficult for a jury to resolve.

The jury was kept for a second night as it carefully considered the case's charges, testimony, facts, and exhibits. When the jury returned to

Taken on October 19, 1967, in Meridian, Mississippi, this photograph shows Deputy Cecil Price (in hat) leaving the Federal Building. Seven women and five men deliberated Price's fate. Price refused to speak publicly about the civil rights workers' murders. But time proved to change Price's racist attitude. In a 1977 *New York Times* magazine interview, he said of integration, "We've got to accept this is the way things are going to be and that's it."

the courtroom on the morning of October 20, foreman Langdon Smith delivered a sealed verdict to Judge Cox.

THE VERDICT

Judge Cox quickly scanned the papers on which the verdict appeared, then handed them to his clerk, who read aloud, "We, the jury, find the defendant Cecil Ray Price not guilty. I'm sorry, your honor, may I start over?" The look on Price's face must have been utter disbelief as the clerk continued, "We, the jury, find the defendant Cecil Ray Price guilty of the charges contained in the indictment." The rest of the defendants braced themselves as the clerk recited the remainder of the verdicts.

Found guilty were Cecil Price, Jimmy Arledge, Sam Bowers, Wayne Roberts, Jimmie Snowden, Billy Wayne Posey, and Horace Doyle Barnette. Found not guilty were Bernard Akin, Lawrence Rainey, Olen Burrage, Frank Herndon, Richard Willis, Herman Tucker, Travis Barnette, and James Harris. The jury was not able to reach a decision for Edgar Ray Killen, Jerry McGrew Sharpe, or Ethel "Hop" Barnett.

Of the seven men convicted of conspiring to deny Mickey Schwerner, James Chaney, and Andrew Goodman their civil rights, Roberts and Bowers were sentenced to ten years in prison; Posey and Price received six-year prison sentences; and Barnette, Snowden, and Arledge each received three years. Incidentally, James Jordan, the prosecution witness who pleaded guilty to his part in the crime, was tried in an Atlanta federal court, where the judge imposed upon him a four-year sentence.

Never before had a jury convicted white men for civil rights violations or the slaying of a black man in the state of Mississippi. The *Meridian Star* newspaper referred to October 20 as "the day the Justice Department broke its losing streak . . . and wrote a new page in Mississippi history."

After unsuccessful appeal bids by each of the convicted Klansmen, the seven guilty men entered federal custody on March 19, 1970.

GLOSSARY

appeal   A request for a new trial.

civil rights   The fundamental freedoms and privileges guaranteed by the Thirteenth and Fourteenth Amendments to the U.S. Constitution and by subsequent acts of Congress, including civil liberties, due process, equal protection of the laws, and freedom from discrimination.

conspiracy   An agreement between two or more people to commit an illegal act.

electoral process   The act of participating in the selection of an elected official; voting for a political candidate.

klavern   A local organizational unit of the Ku Klux Klan.

Ku Klux Klan   A secret society organized in the South after the Civil War to reassert white supremacy by means of terrorism.

lynch   To execute without due process of law, especially to hang, as by a mob.

mistrial   A trial that is invalid due to incorrect procedure or the failure of a jury to reach a verdict.

segregation   The policy or practice of separating people of different races, classes, or ethnic groups, as in schools, housing, and public or commercial facilities, especially as a form of discrimination.

vigilante   One who takes or advocates the taking of law enforcement into one's own hands.

FOR MORE INFORMATION

FREEDOM SUMMER MURDERS
On June 21, 1964, voting rights activists James Chaney, Andrew Goodman, and Michael Schwerner, who had come here to investigate the burning of Mt. Zion Church, were murdered. Victims of a Klan conspiracy, their deaths provoked national outrage and led to the first successful federal prosecution of a civil rights case in Mississippi.

National Association for the Advancement of Colored People (NAACP)
4805 Mount Hope Drive
Baltimore, MD 21215
(877) 622-2798
Web site: http://www.naacp.org

National Civil Rights Museum
450 Mulberry Street
Memphis, TN 38103
(901) 521-9699
Web site: http://www.civilrightsmuseum.org

WEB SITES

Due to the changing nature of Internet links, the Rosen Publishing Group, Inc., has developed an online list of Web sites related to the subject of this book. This site is updated regularly. Please use this link to access the list:

http://www.rosenlinks.com/gttc/mibt

FOR FURTHER READING

Cagin, Seth, and Philip Dray. *We Are Not Afraid: The Story of Goodman, Schwerner, and Chaney and the Civil Rights Campaign for Mississippi*. New York: Macmillian Publishing Company, 1988.

Curtis, Christopher Paul. *The Watsons Go to Birmingham—1963*. New York: Random House Books for Young Readers, 2000.

Fireside, Harvey. *The Mississippi Burning Civil Rights Murder Conspiracy Trial: A Headline Court Case*. Berkeley Heights, NJ: Enslow Publishers, 2002.

Huie, William Bradford. *Three Lives for Mississippi*. Jackson, MS: University Press of Mississippi, 2000.

Levine, Ellen. *Freedom's Children: Young Civil Rights Activists Tell Their Own Stories*. New York: Penguin Putnam Books for Young Readers, 2000.

Mars, Florence. *Witness at Philadelphia*. Baton Rouge, LA: Louisiana University Press, 1976.

Meltzer, Milton. *There Comes a Time: The Struggle for Civil Rights*. New York: Random House Books for Young Readers, 2002.

Rothschild, Mary Aickin. *A Case of Black and White: Northern Volunteers and Southern Freedom Summers*. Westport, CT: Greenwood Press, 1982.

BIBLIOGRAPHY

Cagin, Seth, and Philip Dray. *We Are Not Afraid: The Story of Goodman, Schwerner, and Chaney and the Civil Rights Campaign for Mississippi.* New York: Macmillian Publishing Company, 1988.

Huie, William Bradford. *Three Lives for Mississippi.* Jackson, MS: University Press of Mississippi, 2000.

Linder, Douglas O. "The Mississippi Burning Trial (*U.S. v. Price et al.*)." Retrieved August 2002 (http://www.law.umkc.edu/faculty/projects/ftrials/price&bowers/Account.html).

Minor, Bill. "Yet hearing different drummer, James Meredith returns to UM." Retrieved October 2002 (http://www.clarionledger.com/news/0209/29/lminor.html).

Original FBI Investigation Summary. "MIBURN." Retrieved August 2002 (http://foia.fbi.gov/miburn.htm).

Original Supreme Court Decision. "*United States v. Price et al.*" Retrieved September 2002 (http://www.law.umkc.edu/faculty/projects/ftrials/price&bowers/sctdecision.html).

Original Trial Transcript Excerpts. "*United States v. Price et al.*" Retrieved September/October 2002 (http://www.law.umkc.edu/faculty/projects/ftrials/price&bowers/transcript.html).

PRIMARY SOURCE IMAGE LIST

Cover and page 40: Poster of missing civil rights workers. Created on June 29, 1964, in Washington, D.C.

Page 4: Photograph of plaque commemorating freedom summer murders. Taken on June 17, 1999, in Philadelphia, Mississippi, by an Associated Press photographer.

Page 8: Photograph of Lyndon Baines Johnson.

Page 9: Photograph of a restaurant sit-in. Taken on July 9, 1963, in Cambridge, Maryland.

Page 10: Photograph of freedom riders and burning bus. Taken on May 14, 1961, in Anniston, Alabama. Map of freedom ride locations. From 1961. Housed in the Library of Congress.

Page 13: Photograph of Paul Johnson, John Doar, James Meredith, and James McShane. Taken by Flip Schulke in Oxford, Mississippi, on September 26, 1962.

Page 15: Photograph of civil rights activist teaching new voters. Taken by Flip Schulke in Alabama, circa 1965.

Page 18: Photograph of Michael Schwerner. Distributed by the FBI on June 29, 1964, and reproduced by an Associated Press photographer.

Page 20: Photograph of James Chaney. Taken in Meridian, Mississippi, circa 1960.

Page 22: Photograph of Andrew Goodman. Taken in Oxford, Ohio, on June 15, 1964.

Page 26: Photographs of Herman Tucker, Olen Burrage, Jimmie Snowden, and Bernard Akin. Taken on December 4, 1964, in Jackson, Mississippi.

Page 27: Photographs of Cecil Price, Lawrence Rainey, Jimmy Lee Townsend, and Billy Wayne Posey. Taken on December 4, 1964, in Jackson, Mississippi.

Page 28: Photograph of Edgar Ray Killen. Taken on December 4, 1964, in Jackson, Mississippi.

Page 33: Photograph of Lawrence Rainey, a bodyguard, E. L. McDaniel, and Robert Shelton at a Ku Klux Klan rally. Taken in Merdian, Mississippi, on July 10, 1965.

Page 38: Photograph of the burned CORE station wagon. Taken in Philadelphia, Mississippi, on June 24, 1964.

Page 41: Photograph of excavation site at Old Jolly Farm. Taken on August 5, 1964, near Philadelphia, Mississippi.

Page 42: Photograph of Aaron Henry, Fanny Hamer, and Mr. and Mrs. Schwerner. Taken in Atlantic City, New Jersey, on August 24, 1964.

Page 43: Photograph of investigators in swamp around Philadelphia, Mississippi. Taken on June 24, 1964.

Page 45: Photograph of John Doar taken by Francis Miller in September 1962 in Oxford, Mississippi.

Page 48: Photograph of Cecil Price and Lawrence Rainey at their arraignment. Taken on December 5, 1964, in Meridian, Mississippi.

Page 51: Photograph of Edgar Ray Killen entering court. Taken on October 12, 1967, in Meridian, Mississippi.

Page 54: Photograph of Cecil Price leaving court. Taken on October 19, 1967, in Meridian, Mississippi.

INDEX

FREEDOM SUMMER MURDERS

On June 21, 1964, voting rights activists James Chaney, Andrew Goodman, and Michael Schwerner, who had come here to investigate the burning of Mt. Zion Church, were murdered. Victims of a Klan conspiracy, their deaths provoked national outrage and led to the first successful federal prosecution of a civil rights case in Mississippi.

Donated by the listeners of WRXL, Jackson, MS

ABOUT THE AUTHOR

A diverse freelance writer, Bill Scheppler has written on subjects ranging from the Internet to the Ironman, from Special Forces to civil rights. *The Mississippi Burning Trial* is Bill's fourth book for the Rosen Publishing Group.

CREDITS

Cover, pp. 1, 9, 10 (top), 20, 22, 26-27, 28, 33, 40, 41, 42, 48, 51, 54 © Bettmann/Corbis; pp. 4, 18, 38, 43, © AP/Wide World Photos; p. 8 Prints and Photographs Division, Library of Congress; p. 10 (bottom) Geography and Maps Division, Library of Congress; pp. 13, 15 © Flip Schulke/Corbis; p. 45 © Timepix.

Designer: Les Kanturek; **Editor:** Christine Poolos